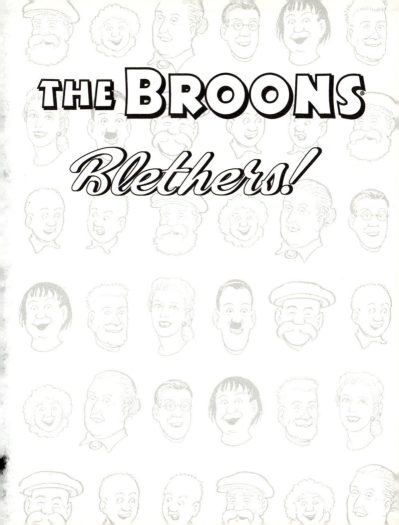

THE BROONS

Blethers!

THE BROONS

Blethers!

Rib-tickling Words and Phrases
From Scotland's Favourite Family

BLACK & WHITE PUBLISHING

First published 2015
by Black & White Publishing Ltd
29 Ocean Drive, Edinburgh EH6 6JL

1 3 5 7 9 10 8 6 4 2   15 16 17 18

ISBN: 978 1 910230 24 4

The Broons® ©DC Thomson & Co. Ltd. 2015
www.thebroons.com

Text by Euan Kerr

A CIP catalogue record for this book is available from the British Library.

Typeset by 3btype.com
Printed and bound in Poland by www.hussarbooks.pl

Introduction

Perhaps this book is a little late . . . about 80 years late! The Broons cartoon strip first appeared in *The Sunday Post* newspaper in 1936, depicting the humorous trials and tribulations of the residents of 10 Glebe Street. The large family all speak in the Scottish vernacular using words and phrases that only home-grown Scots would be likely to understand.

At long last, using the brilliant drawings of the original artist, Dudley D. Watkins, to help illustrate the meanings, we try to explain just what some of these baffling words and phrases actually mean.

Hope you find it stappit fu' of fun!

Shoot the craw

Depart rapidly

Whit a minter

How frightfully embarrassing

Daft galloots

Foolish fellows

Goin' their dingers

Expostulating vehemently

Heavin'

Overcrowded

Fly auld chancers

Wily old opportunists

Couped

Fallen over

Wallies

False teeth

Hoachin' wi' Folk

Rather overcrowded

Sneckin'

Acquiring dishonestly

Pechin'

Out of breath

Tattie howkin'

Harvesting potatoes manually

Keekin'

Peeping

Zonked oot

In a deep sleep

Hud yer wheesht

Do be quiet

Lang streak o' misery

Tall, unimposing chap

Haein' a rumble

Engaging in fisticuffs

Black affronted

Utterly ashamed

Gie's a piece

Give me a sandwich

Gie's peace

Do be quiet

Winchin'

Courting

Steak an' ingans

Steak and onions

Feart

In trepidation

Whit a stooshie

What a hullabaloo

Scaffies

Refuse collectors

Shoogle

Shake violently

Stoor

Dust

Crivvens!

I say!

Nippit

Tight

Fly wee beesom

Cunning little monkey

Mawkit

Scruffy

Heedrum-hodrum

Scottish music

Guisin'

Dressing up for Hallowe'en

Gie'n them pelters

Expressing angry abuse

Clatter intae

Collide Forcefully

Stoatin' doon

Raining heavily

Clootie Dumpling

Fruit pudding cooked in cloth

Caught bonnie

Found out

Keepie uppie

Football juggling

Tak a scunner to

A strong dislike of

Stappit Fu'

Replete

Hoochter Teuchter music

Scottish country dancing

Crabbit auld wifies

Ill-tempered elderly ladies

Awfie peely wally

Rather pale and sickly looking

Feechie

Most unpleasant

Hoose lookin' like a midden

Home looking like a refuse tip

Gowpin'

Looking astounded

Fankled

Somewhat entangled

Haein' a spree

Having a party

Bonnie fechters

Skilled combatants

Gie'n it laldy

Giving all you've got

Bampot

Imbecile

Twa clicks for ye

Two boyfriends for you

Scunnered

Extremely fed up

Totally minted

Wealthy beyond belief

Sleekit

Cunning

Spyl't rotten

Made something of a fuss over

Mony a mickle maks a muckle

Thriftness is a virtue

Steamie

Public wash-house

Sair bahoochie

Painful posterior

Lumber

Romantic partner

In their scratcher

Abed

Cuddy

Horse

Puir wee sowels

Unfortunate little chaps

Peuchy

Revolting

Clippie

Bus conductor

Drookit

Wet through

Done up tae the nines

A little overdressed

A puckle neeps

A few turnips

Chappin'

Unable to play at dominoes
or powerless to continue

Clarty bunnet

Soiled headgear

Mixter maxter

Confused jumble

Whit a reek

What an unpleasant, smokey smell

Trauchled

Worn out with overwork

Skinny malinky lang legs

Tall gangly person

Cuddyback riding

Pony trekking

Gubbed

Defeated

Poor oot

Wedding scramble

Dookin' fur apples

A bit o' a rammy

Hopscotch

Peevers

Dunfoonert

Flabbergasted

Birling along!

Running at speed

In a state of confusion

In a Fankle

Skite

Slip Forcefully

Wee bauchle

Small, unimposing chap

Apple bobbing